Death & Rapture

in the Animal Kingdom

Also by Norah Pollard

Leaning In (poems & CD)

Report from the Banana Hospital (poems & CD)

Geisha (illustrations)

Death & Rapture
in the Animal Kingdom

Poems by

Norah Pollard

Antrim House
Simsbury, Connecticut

Copyright © 2009 by Norah Pollard

Except for short selections reprinted for purposes of
book review, all reproduction rights are reserved.
Requests for permission to replicate should
be addressed to the publisher.

Library of Congress Control Number: 2008939542

ISBN 978-0-9798451-3-0

Printed & bound by United Graphics, Inc.

First Edition, 2009

Cover Art: Sandy Mastroni

Photograph of author: Sue Carr

Book Design: Rennie McQuilkin

Antrim House
860.217.0023
AntrimHouse@comcast.net
www.AntrimHouseBooks.com
P.O. Box 111, Tariffville, CT 06081

for Michael

Acknowledgements

I wish to acknowledge my great debt to my parents for giving me the best education a writer could have. Glad thanks to my mother for reading to me each night all through my childhood until she was hoarse—reading everything from "Baa-baa, Black Sheep," "Three Little Kittens," " Little Black Sambo" and "The Gingerbread Man" to Goldsmith's "An Elegy on the Death of a Mad Dog" and Kingsley's *Water Babies*; and to my father, for sitting at the kitchen table nights with his glass of Four Roses, talking seriously to me about the Finnegan fairies, the brownies and the "least leprechauns," and reciting in his fine deep voice long passages from such poems as "The Rubáiyát," Burns' "John Anderson, My Jo," Gray's "Elegy," Leigh Hunt's "Jenny Kissed Me," "The Rime of the Ancient Mariner" (of course), "Evangeline," and "To An Athlete Dying Young." I remember all the stories, Momma. I remember all the poems, Donkey Dust, my Dad.

And my very deep gratitude to Rennie McQuilkin, without whose strong encouragement I would not have continued, and without whose honest and fine criticism I would not have continued nearly as well. Blessings on you, Rennie—my mentor, my friend.

Table of Contents

NORAH

The Doll	15
What Poets Know	17
Izmir	19
The Dance	22
Recension	23
The Great Chicken Leg Incident	25
Grace	28
26, That Son-of-a-Bitch	29
Crossroads	31
The Feroleto Steel Receptionist	33
Song of the Sweet-Ass Lover	35
Mnemonic	36
Signals	37
Midwinter Visit Home	39
Goodbye, Goodbye, Sweet Dreams	41
She Dreamed of Cows	43
Death & Rapture in the Animal Kingdom	44
Willy's Feathers	46
Lion	48
Silence, the Old One's Gift	50
Church	51
A Word from the Universe	52
Prophecy from the Interior	53

MICHAEL

Rush	57

The Physics of Contingency	59
In Recovery	60
The Sum of a Man	62
Say Goodbye, Say It Without Angels	64
In a Blind Hour	65
What Is Lost	68
Prayer for my Brother	70
Pleasure Beach	72

JIM

Jimmie and the Moongirl	77
Jimmie Full in the Belly	79
Fly Fishing	81
Marlboro Van Man	83
Buddha in the Bottle, Buddha in the Van	84
He Is The River	85
A Good Day	87
Lake Lillinonah	89
The Birdcatcher	92
The Bird	94
Rain	97
A Woman in Love	100
I Lie in Wonder	102
West Wind	103
St. Valentine's Day	105
Not Happiness but Something Else	106
His Anger	107
The Spell	109
One Man	110
Ice	111

ABOUT THE AUTHOR	115

Sometimes I go about pitying myself. And all the while I am being carried on great winds across the sky.

– Ojibwa

We are also what we have lost.

– Juno Gemes

Death & Rapture
in the Animal Kingdom

Norah

The Doll

Almost a stranger now, my father comes
out of the winter cold with gifts.
Mine, a carnival doll, so ravishing a thing—
the big red velvet hat with white feather plumes,
the painted brows arched in continuous surprise,
the red bowed lips, the abundant orange hair,
the rhinestone earrings nailed to her ears.
The eyes are green glass and open and shut
like bivalves.

Her gown is velvet also, crimson with yellow
tasseling, long skirt flowing, but underneath
—a shock like finding a dead pet—
nothing below the waist. A blank.
No belly. No mousey. No legs. No feet.
Just crimson velvet, flowing.

My father, haggard from his long journey, has gone
to bed alone in the leftover greying light, and my mother,
terse and stiff (he's brought presents but not money),
is sitting by the window jabbing her needle into
the mending.

The house is quiet and cold, and no supper coming.
I will take my doll to show Ann around the block.
We'll imagine castles and steeds and ladies-in-waiting
and my doll will be the queen.

No one has seen such a doll in Pawtucket.
Annie will envy me.

I shiver and call at Annie's back door.
She opens and stares at the doll with no name
(I know no name grand enough to name her)
and says in an unimpressed voice, "I can't come out."
"I have a new doll," I say. I hold her up. Annie shrugs.
"It's Lucien's feast day."
I can hear singing, and the laughter of her brother.
Someone is playing an accordion. She looks back
towards the kitchen, smiles down at her feet
and shuts the door.

Oh, what can I tell you of the heart of a girl
carrying a harlot-haired doll across an empty
winter schoolyard, the swings stirring slightly
in a weak wind,
no trees, no sun, no birdsong,
only cold stones in the schoolyard, everything grey,
and a scarlet doll in her arms.

What Poets Know

I come from a long line of men.
Even my mother was a man—
broad-shouldered, strong of mind, untender.
My father and his father and my
father's brothers were seamen and
boxers and hunters and riders.
They drank to death without any
dainty constraints, and they smoked,
snorted and chewed tobacco until
their lungs were black as coal hods
and their black teeth laughed
like the black keys on a piano.
Ah, and they did laugh!

And weep!
When a man wept it was because a woman
gave him trouble. (Because women
could whip them with lilies, and bring them
to kneel with the beauty of their scorn.)
Then they'd weep and drink and drive
out to the hills to hunt cougar,
roar back home, eat fried hornpout,
and shout about their kill.

Me, I learned to be silent.
I'd wade the Ten Mile River,

search the woods for traps to spring,
eat mulberries, chew on mint, collect snakeskins.
By night I'd sit by the falls and watch
the stars bounce around in the plunge pool.
At home I dreamed, sat alone, was
forgotten and unaddressed.
I fell into the condition of poetry.
I was one on whom nothing was lost.
I saw, I heard, and my head
was full of light and visions.
It made my reason delicate.

Now, on dark nights,
I'll dance with gentle death in the orchard
while men at home, in barns, in pubs,
swear and laugh and rut and snore.

And the moon shines on.
And death is a woman.

Izmir

I lived in the hills that year. The Aegean lay below
and the brown and rusted mountains rose up behind.
The air so clear you saw three, four, five dimensions
of everything—a shrike in its long drop from the sky,
a lone cypress, the hut on the next hill, all as distinct
as pop-up figures in a children's book.
The undulations of the silver green olive leaves
caused the grove to look ambulant, as though it were
moving up the mountain like a herd.
Sometimes a man would come trudging down the hill
in his cloth cap, baggy pants, the enduring rifle
slung over his shoulder, barrel sticking up
like a narrow wing.
Shepherds in their large cloaks and hoods stood in
the middle of the grazing sheep, their transistor radios
pressed to their ears. Black nights, I could hear
the *bekçis'* whistle carrying thinly through the hills
as they signaled one another all is well.

I was twenty-three and sick and far from home.
Hepatitis, dysentery, and who-knows-what
My body thin, and thinner. The skin a curious
sallow yellow. My long hair fell out in swatches
on my pillow, so I covered my head with scarves.
What little I ate ran through my body.
I wore diapers and rinsed them in the tub.
I felt drunk all the time. Once, weaving and

staggering, trying to make it from the stove
to the chair, I had a laughing fit. I sat
on the floor and laughed until I fell asleep
against the wall.

Dozing and drifting, at times the thought would come
that I might die there in the hills outside of Izmir.
I was oddly unconcerned, though dying struck me as
ill-advised. (How would they get my body home?
What about my things?)
All fall, nerveless and listless, I would lie out on
the balcony watching the large tortoises shambling
down from the hill. I saw the early mists roll around
the tops of the mountains. I could see British ships
in the harbor dwarfing the gaily colored two-eyed
fishing boats. I could make out the palms glittering
along the quay. I drank chai and ate pine nuts and tried
to eat the lumpy, horny-skinned yogurt Gonca sent up.
And I watched my body disappearing from me.

Winter came. I could not keep warm. My periods
stopped. My breasts melted back into my chest.
I said aloud to no one, "Soon I will be back in the womb."
One morning, shivering, I threw off the blankets and
looked down at my perfectly articulated ribs, my
hips thrusting up from my flesh like axes,
the knobs of my knees, my pubis jutting up and hairless,
and I wept for myself.

Months after months of dreaming, drifting, then spring.
The yogurt and the fresh peanut butter Gonca had fed me
all winter helped my hair grow back.
Flickers of energy. One day the almond trees glowed pink
with flowers. The next day I saw two fawns. And the next
I put Gonca's metal bowls in a filet and started slowly down
the steep path to her place. I stopped to poke at a baby snake
and smiled at the return of curiosity.

Then, halfway down the hill, I stumbled. To keep upright
I needed to take huge steps—and because of the steepness—faster,
longer steps, and soon I was running downhill simply to keep
upright, running, pots and bowls clanging like a runaway
trolley, baby hair winging, so weightless, so light, so bodiless,
running, not running, flying down the hill without strength
or will to stop myself. Laughing and flying and feeling
my body borne along by its lightness, flying and clanging,
clanging and laughing, flying but in long lopes touching down,
returning to the pull of the earth,
clanging and laughing.

The Dance

Night,
snow pending,
I stop to look
through the lighted window
of the dance instruction school
where the dancers stand stalled,
holding one another stiff as dolls
waiting for instructions, or music perhaps,
beautiful in their expectancy.
One woman—spine arched, head flung back,
black hair streaming—is looking
through the frosted window
north into the night.
A thin cold wind blows steadily.
Ice glitters on the telephone lines
and gleams around the pink neon sign:
"Leon's Ballroom Dancing."

A whispering snow begins to fall, and
just now the couples begin to move
in twirling circles of blue, gold and green,
in silence soundless as a dream.
Looking in at their lit loveliness from
an empty night and cold,
my bag of bread stiffening in the chill,
I hear the Naugatuck Valley freight
drag its moan across the silvering town.
I hurry home, alone.

Recension

Hate, rage, bitterness—words
that don't belong in a poem.
Yet I'll write here how—
my finger at the trigger,
my knife at your fat throat—
I've killed you many hundred times
in dreams.

You almost broke me.
I'd go round and round those sorrow rooms
whispering to myself old songs,
chanting rhymes from my childhood,
mumbling voices of my lost home,
ghost trying to call myself back.

All that was long ago, yet
I can't forget.
I've cried out in the night
the only prayer I know,
"Unbitter me!"
Who is it hears? And it's been years.

But yesterday,
as I was choosing apples at the grocer's,
I saw you—broad hunched shoulders,
jacket hitched behind, standing
with your back to me

by the stall of pale turnips, winter squash,
cauliflower white as bridal flowers.
And—reflexively as reaching out
to catch the bride's bouquet—
my heart leapt high and gay
with an instant's ignorant joy.
You turned—it was not you.
And I remembered who you have become.

But that flash of joy!
I did love you once.
This much is true.

The Great Chicken Leg Incident

On his plate, broccoli, smashed potatoes, and
a stricken chicken leg. The boy sits sullen as a possum.
"Why do we always have to have chicken leg?" he asks,
tapping his fork on his plate.
She says, "Eat your dinner," hard hours spent at work
and the heat of the kitchen in her words.
"Chicken legs are gross," he seethes. His mother sighs.
While she gazes tiredly around the table for
the salt, he slides his fork tines under the chicken
and hits the handle hard.

The leg flips across the salad, hits the gravy boat and
skids two yards across the linoleum. It leaves a greasy line
like snail's slime. The boy's sister sucks in her breath.
No one speaks. The mother rises up, retrieves
the crusty leg, places it with exaggerated carefulness
on his plate, and says low and through her teeth,
"If you ever do that again, I will wipe your face with it."

She sits as though strung on wires. Savagely butters her bread.
Seven beats. The boy begins to hum "Rhinestone Cowboy."
He swings his feet. He casually leans on his elbow.
The fork casually inches out, eases under the leg, and
he launches it.

The leg in the air, the leg in the air, the leg arcing, twisting,
pitchpoling, the leg descending, the leg exploding

in the kitty box, litter flying like buckshot.
Then that stillness, as after the lava solidified on Pompeii.

The girl is transfixed. The boy alert, red, jittery, a smile
playing on his face. The mother rises, being a woman of
her word. She pulls the leg out of the clumped litter and
picks the litter off with extravagant delicacy.

And then they're on the floor. The leg in his ear.
Under the table. The leg down his neck. Oily bits.
Alley oop. Under the chair, greasing his eyes.
Half nelson. Fat gobbets. Hip toss. Down around
the trash bin. The leg under his pants. Tiger driver.
The crusty pimpled chicken leg everywhere at once.
Golden boyhead. Mother eyeflash. Sister pulling
her knees to her chest. Boy half sobbing, but almost
laughing. Mother on the floor, hair in greasy strings,
wielding a chicken leg like a caveman's club.

It is finished. They stand panting. His hair sticks out
in peaks. He glows with grease-shine and fury.
"Now go and take a shower," the mother says,
pointing like God.
And does he?
Of course not.
With her last bit of strength she catches him up by his shirt,
pulls and pounds him, thrashing, up the stairs,
flings him in the shower like a bag of eels.

Fifteen, twenty, twenty-five minutes, the mother
chewing determinedly the cold green beans and
the girl watching her tensely. The sound of gallons
of water glugging down the pipes in the walls
like the laugh of a loony. Finally the girl says
in a half-whisper, "I don't think he's going to come out."
"No," says the mother.
She lays down her fork, takes off her apron, lifts
her sweater from the hook, says, "I'll be walking."
And out the door.

She stumps along through the field, lungs clenched up,
breathing shallow with anger. Getting up through
the pine grove, then slowing, then wandering along
Shore Road until she comes to the river.
And does she throw herself in?
Drown herself just thinking of the teenage years ahead?
Of course not.

She takes a long deep drink of the night air. A little curling
smile tugs one side of her mouth. She stands looking out at the
rustling river, seeing not the river but that magnificent
stubbornness, his shining gold-greased self,
that fire in his eye.
She turns home.

Grace

The big dead Christmas turkey
cooked three weeks ago and 1/3 eaten,
offering a whiff of graveolence and
filling up the fridge with the ghost of itself
is carried out in the dark and tossed on the pile
of needles under the pine in the backyard
for the skunk, the raccoon and the opossum.

All night they do their job. In the morning
the squirrels are two-stepping around it,
having pulled it out to middle yard.
The crows wait respectfully at some distance,
shuffling and angling,
and when the squirrels are finished
hop to it, drag it, pick it, strip it, lift it,
make it fly a foot from where it was.
The littler birds are last, but they make a day of it.
Flutter, stamp, fly, gnaw, chew, peck, pull.

Over the days the turkey carcass,
like the skeletal hull of a ship,
floats around the yard.
Every time I look out the window
it's in a different spot until
the day when there is nothing there at all.
The turkey has gone elsewhere.
We remain.
For this, we all give thanks.

26, That Son-of-a-Bitch

is the number she gives me
to stand in the unemployment line—
25 people before me—
when all I want is the yellow form
which rests in a wooden slot
by her left hand.

"It's right there." I point
to the slip of paper she could have
handed me, but won't—
"You have to wait your turn
like everyone else." The voice
of a smug-ass crow. There is a
shivering in her eyes like skatebugs
agitating water, and her mouth
hoists up in one corner like the flap
of a tent.
She hitches up her bra straps,
aims her great breasts at me.
Cuts me down.

The cheap plastic seat
shaped like the palm of a hand
holds my butt
while rage does its nasty St. Vitus
in my chest.
I watch the poor, the slack, the
skinny, the fat, the desperate,
the boy with the tattoo *Loser*

on his forehead, the green-haired girl
with the small cross dangling from her nose.
And I think,
Who am I? Who am I
to be enraged?

So I try to sit quietly, court serenity.
I think of night.
I think of stars, and forests, and
seas. I think of graves.
I try.
But my eye keeps flying back
like a ball on elastic
to the fat woman at the counter
controlling Time like God,
until I snap, uprise,
mambo up to her jumbo judgment desk,
lean in between the unmanned unemployed
turret lathe operator (# 33)
and her bomb-nosed boobs,
snatch the yellow form
and boogie out
amid her shout,
the big **26**,
badge of we poor with huddled asses,
pressed tight against
my indigent heart.

Crossroads

I have a cross on lay-a-way
at the ABC Jewelry Store
in Bridgeport
where the Chinese owners
sell gold tooth jackets
and names like *Hawk* and *Jo-Jo*
spelled out in diamonds across
gold knuckle-dusters.
From black velvet cards, gold earrings hang
immense as CD's, and industrial size chains
dangle gold tigers with ruby eyes
or emerald-scaled snakes in striking mode
or the white-enamel-eyed agonized Jesus.

In Delia's Dreams ("Nothing over $9.99!")
hip-hop blares through fluorescent strobes.
Silk sequined bras, striped red stockings
and crystal power beads jitter with the bass.
The music jumps my blood, makes me choose
a leopard satin jumpsuit. In the fitting room,
inside the leopard's satin skin,
I slink before the mirror, flash my nails.
A low snarl surprises me.

Outside Sanjay's Luncheonette
a mustachioed man sits all day on a milk crate
smoking cheroots. He's selling "oriental" rugs

with pink and black zebra stripes or fleshy nudes
that loll amid green grapes, black roses.
A blind man at the corner, all bones,
plays "Bad Case of Love" on the clarinet.

Perry, the shy-smiling Chinese boy
at ABC who hardly speaks,
records the payment carefully
for my cross of faux diamonds—
very wide, Byzantinely curved,
heavy with longing, attitude,
and disbelief.

The Feroleto Steel Company Receptionist

The middle-aged receptionist
sleeping at the phone
or working the crosswords like her fate
when she's awake
is me.
Sometimes I'll file my fingernails.
It's expected.
Sometimes I'll look at the pictures
from the coffee table magazines—
*New Steel, American Metal Market,
Modern Metals.*

My face, never much,
is jowly now,
the creampuff breasts are crêpes,
and I've a wattle.
But my voice and my legs—
that's what I had, and
that's what I've got.
After 31 years you'd think
I'd answer automatic as Pavlov's dog.
But I pull out of me, "Feroleto Steel,
may I help?" all curious and
honeyed with sex,
a saxophone voice,

and I make you feel good for calling.
My tongue says "steel" but you hear
skin, good whiskey,
harmonicas and money.

Song of the Sweet-Ass Lover

No one really talks about sex, so most of us
go through life not really knowing
of its strangeness—
its varieties, its vagaries,
its antic behaviories.

But most women get around to
learning on their own that
some men jump up after sex
and take a shower,
some men roll away and light a cigarette,
and some just fall asleep hard
and leave you all alone thinking about
the Ice Capades or the plumber's green pants.

But once I loved a man who, after the little death,
the sweet lostness, the divine posterial sneeze,
would cry out near tears, "Hold me! Please!
Hold me! Ah, God! Hold me down!"

Which—Ah, God!—I would.

Mnemonic

When I walk up Chopsey Hill
toward the great blue pine,
its branches full of hidden nests
and secretive birds,
I fix my eyes on the pine's peak so
as I come nearer and nearer,
my eyes toward the sky,
the pine seems to be slowly
falling on me.

Then from deep inside,
my heart blasts out of its
old pocket under my ribs
and my lungs cram with laughter.
The low needled branches rake my hair.
Birds skitter in the boughs.
Some of them hoo.

I do this each time I go up Chopsey Hill—
my eyes fasten on the pine's peak,
the tree falls on me, my heart
jumps hard and wide.
I do this to sense again how I feel
when you first come over me to make love—
just that same wild bloom of awe and joy,
your shoulders, your chest darkening the world
like night coming down,
your face, your shadowed eyes.
Small birds rustling in your hair.

Signals

St. John the Baptist Greek Cemetery, Stratford

At the top of Nichols Hill
is a small domed chapel
hemmed by four tall spindling pines.
The wind blows sweet and free
through the uncut grass.
It is night. The few birds in the
four lean trees sing their quiet elegies.
Under the moon, the chapel's dome
glows like a sister moon.

Cascading from the chapel
higgledy-piggledy all around the hill
sprawl the gravestones.
Greek and Russian crosses top each stone,
stark white against the darkening sky.
Here and there beside a grave a candle flame
wavers softly in its red glass lamp
like a tongue in a mouth.
The dead look steadily into the night
from photographs set in the granite.

In the dark, the polished stones
are picked out by headlights
circling the road around Nichols Hill.
All night the gravestones flare—

some gleam high, some low.
Three or four or nine will flash at once.

On darkest nights, I'll
flash back my high beams,
acknowledging the invitation.

Midwinter Visit Home

I

This is the street where my parents lived,
theirs, this basic, graceless squat white house.
Lacking sidewalks, it always looked as if it might be vacant,
nor is there tree or lighted lamp to soften things.
Now, one forgotten summer awning on the second floor
flaps in the greying evening's wind—
a tattered flag over the cold and empty camp.

II

My parents were always cold.
They searched the South for warmth in winter months
until it had gotten cold there, too, they said,
and in their later years did not go.
So she made pots of acrid tea against the chill
and sat straight up to take her cup,
while in a farther room he drank his brandy neat
while watching warmer lives played out on the TV.
But through the distance of their rooms
they shared a grudge
he could not fathom, nor she explain.

III

This is the place where my parents lie,
down in the dark at the very end of their street—
in a common hole, an economical Rhode Island grave.
The gates are open still.
I find their basic, squat grey stone—
an ordinary grave in rows of hundreds—
and stand on the hard ground where she
is stacked on top of him, the cold connection.
I stand over them, on them,
wishing my love could warm them like a sun.
Marveling
that the ground can contain their rage,
that their piece of earth does not crack and yaw,
spit huge flames of fury
to leap high into this night and blacken the moon—
a bonfire big enough to scorch New England's winter,
fueled with the ore of their baffled, unending ire.

Goodbye, Goodbye, Sweet Dreams

for Barbara Jennings

Dark in your room. No one visits.
I put the light on,
wake you with *Hello! Hello!*
calling your name loudly as if
you were down a deep hole.
Reluctantly your lids open and you drag
your focus back to this world, and to me,
but with eyes turned wild with such
imprisoned rage I retreat from you,
run to the nurse's station, ask for
ice chips, Vaseline on a stick, a comb,
and come back armed with a busyness
and moisten your lips and fuss
with your hair, your covers,
while the machines keep up their threshing,
sucking and hissing all around your stone body,
your beautiful purpled hands.

Months and months and months on this black rack.

You can move only your dark eyes,
and tonight you use them, wild as Kabuki,
rolling them first to the pump on your left,
then to me, then to the tubes on your right,
then back to me.

Over and over, you drag those images of life-in-death
to me with fierce intent
and I know, I know
what you are asking.

I know and all I say,
the way you'd talk to a child, is
"You hate these machines, don't you?"
So furiously, then, do you engage me with your eyes
that at last, shaken, I say *Goodbye,*
goodbye, sweet dreams,
I'll be back, I'll be back,
as I wave from the door.
Your eyes fix me in the sights
of your rage and despair as I slip from your room
out into the harsh bright corridors of morality,
lacking the compassion, courage,
or even enough simple love
to do as you wish,
my old friend,
my dear ghost,
my heart's harrow.

She Dreamed of Cows

I knew a woman who washed her hair and bathed
her body and put on the nightgown she'd worn
as a bride and lay down with a .38 in her right hand.
Before she did the thing, she went over her life.
She started at the beginning and recalled everything—
all the shame, sorrow, regret and loss.
This took her a long time into the night
and a long time crying out in rage and grief and disbelief—
until sleep captured her and bore her down.

She dreamed of a green pasture and a green oak tree.
She dreamed of cows. She dreamed she stood
under the tree and the brown and white cows
came slowly up from the pond and stood near her.
Some butted her gently and they licked her bare arms
with their great coarse drooling tongues. Their eyes, wet as
shining water, regarded her. They came closer and began to
press their warm flanks against her, and as they pressed
an almost unendurable joy came over her and
lifted her like a warm wind and she could fly.
She flew over the tree and she flew over the field and
she flew with the cows.

When the woman woke, she rose and went to the mirror.
She looked a long time at her living self.
Then she went down to the kitchen which the sun had made all
yellow, and she made tea. She drank it at the table, slowly,
all the while touching her arms where the cows had licked.

Death & Rapture in the Animal Kingdom

Maybe they don't think of death
the way we do—
as a nothingness, an extinction,
or else a golden place with
access to a God—
but the animals know of dying.

They spend their days in artful vigilance
hiding from the larger tooth, the sharper claw,
evading the shadow of the wing,
ducking the bullet.
The long cold howl of the wolf, the bear's thick stink
float over their days and fog their dreams.

The animals walk in fear through the world.
Fear is their second nature.
But they are not afraid of fear.
Fear gives their days their shining—
the grey river's glint and spark,
the meadow's deep green rolling,
the shadowed sanctuary of trees,
lush rain, luster of sun.

The animals lope and leap
and roll in long grasses

even while ever watching their backs.

The animals know of dying.
Eluding death for one more hour is
their constant paradise.

Willy's Feathers

My little Monk parrot's been dead three months,
and still I find his feathers around the house—
a long green and turquoise tail feather beside the piano,
his lime green down behind the bed and, in
the pink azalea by the door, a blue and weathered
wing feather dangles from the leaves.
Each time I find a feather I kiss it and put it
in a bowl in my room on a desk full of family photos.
Sometimes I weep.

Today an early morning dream brought a thin white wind
like a gauzy spirit sweeping around the room
stirring the curtains, swirling the feathers in the bowl
faster and faster, brighter and brighter until
they came together in a bright green bird,
my bird, Willy's aqua wings, his merry agate eyes!
I woke and for some seconds felt enormous joy.

Then I understood.
I rose and pulled on clothes
and covered the bowl with a blue silk scarf
and carried it out in the cool morning to the woods
where the tall pines grow.
I stood with the pines and waited for
the right morning wind off the river and
when it turned my way I lifted the bowl high
and drew off the scarf.

The wind lifted the feathers from the bowl. Some sailed upwards and settled in the needles, some stuck, little green flags, on the rugged bark, and some swirled and danced and floated high into the sun.

Lion

If I were to fall in love with a lion,
a long-faced, round-eared, black-
mouthed lion,
a handsome, gaily dispositioned lion,
a good gold lion,
I should be able to marry that lion
because I love him.
I should be able to live with him
in his lion's den
and share red meat meals
and sleep within the circle of his
big nailed paws
because I love him.
I should be able to roam the hot savannah
in freedom with my lion.
I should be able to ride on his back
as he lopes to the stream, and watch
while his wide red tongue curls
to scoop the water that smells of sweetgrass.
And while we rest under the baobab,
I should be able to glean the straw and burrs
from his gold mane and remove small splinters
from his great paw pads
because I love him.
When my lion desires me
and I get down on all fours under the shade
of the thorn tree
and feel his great weight on my shoulders

and take his heartseed in me,
I should be able to cry out
in exaltation and gladness,
not secret or ashamed.
I should be able to suckle his young.
And if he is wounded in battle with a buffalo,
I should be able to lick his wounds with my own tongue
and lie beside him to comfort him in his agony
because I love him.
And if he dies, I should be able to grieve
and rake my skin and strike my eyes
because he is the lion I love.
And I should be able to take some hair
from his gold mane and weave it in my own hair
and take some hair of his gold plumed tail
to make a tasseling for my neck,
for this is my inheritance from him.
And I should be able to bear him away
to a secret spot near the green river's bend
where the water splashes lightly over rocks
and sounds like singing.
I should be able to bury him there
where the bushwillow leans over green water
because I am married to my lion.
Because he is my family.
Because I love my lion.

Silence, the Old One's Gift

When I was young, I was so intense.
I couldn't talk fast enough.
My mouth was a canning factory,
my tongue was a train.
To anyone who'd listen, I'd talk about
parrots and estuaries,
religion's hats and rings, the veils of politics.
And, of course, I'd talk about love,
its fleshly extraordinaries,
its tides in the blood.
But mostly, when I was young, I'd talk
about myself—
> *This is what I'm feeling now,*
> *this is what I was feeling then,*
> *this is what I'll be feeling tomorrow*
> *...unless I feel otherwise.*

Years have passed.
I am silent now.
Not that I am wise.
Not that I understand anything.
But when I sit on the back steps at sundown
watching the white pine turn gold
and the cones at its sixty-foot peak
glow yellow, some flashing a crystal
drop of sap at their tip,
there is nothing I need to say to you,
though I will be considering its loveliness
for hours.

Church

An early Sunday morning in January.
I do not go to church
but sit quietly in the grey light, listening.
Silence for a long time.
Then the far-off whistle of the 9:47 Metro-North.
Some time later, the sweet high chimes from
St. Stanislaus float through the trees, and then
minutes later, the faint pop-pop-pop
of the hunters' guns aiming for duck
on Nell's Island.
And all under this cold winter morning
the furnace thrums, faithful
as an old heart.

And there is one other sound—
the throaty purr of the old grey cat.
Surrounded by the rug's rich burgundy and gold guls,
she lies on her back on the worn Bukara,
legs splayed like an old doxy.
I smile for her independent contentment.
I have also heard that cats will purr
to comfort themselves when they're in pain or dying.
The way humans will pray.

A Word from the Universe

October storm moving in,
blowing from the northeast—
winds whipping the clouds to shreds,
the sun above a maroon horizon going down hard,
turning the beach road sycamores a blood red.
The small stilted houses on Russian Beach
flare as though burning from within.
Big gray waves shouldering in
pound the beach where the gulls
sit in groups, still as planted rocks
but for the neck feathers fluttering.
And me on the shore lashed by the wind,
straddle-legged, trying to stay upright,
spray and sand flaying my face.
My great happiness in my nothingness.

Prophecy from the Interior

In a barren place
there is a horse
still standing,
his legs cut off at the knees.
He is still trying to run.
Far away there is
another horse, lying on his side,
his legs, from the knees down,
gone.
Nothing in the sky but blue heat.
Nothing on the ground but blood,
two brown bridleless horses,
sand, and stone.

That is it. The entire dream.
But what would those dream interpreters
of the Pharaoh tell me?
Why am I left with this image
burning my eyes, this riddle
chilling my lips?

It is said that everything
in the dream
is you.

Then I am the wingless, legless horses.
I am the one dying, and

I am the one yet standing.
I am the wild brown animal in the dust,
and I am the beautiful one
still striving to run.
I am the sky and the sand.
I am the rocks and the blood.

MICHAEL

for John Michael Pollard (1945-2006)

Rush

You, on your way to school, your books flung
in the bushes, stand as you have stood every morning
for a week—though in different places—on the tracks
running from Providence through Pawtucket to Worcester,
waiting for the P&W, sensing its coming before you can
see it, the ties under your sneakers beginning so slightly
to shudder, the steel rails' vibrations coming in little
shock waves, the weeds between the ties turning to their
long trembling. The sun glazes three sides of bits of
black coal to silver, and you watch as the 7:35 a mile away
explodes around the bend, headlight shining brighter than
the morning, whistle blasting the sleep from the homes
on each wrong side of the tracks, the engineer seeing again
the apparition he's been seeing for a week—a too-thin boy,
arms by his side, chin up, a wraith with palomino hair.

The engineer leans way out, waving one arm and pulling
on the screaming whistle, and the engineer himself screaming,
a half mile, a quarter, a fifth, until you and he can now
see one another's eyes, the engineer still trying to brake,
the wheels screeching, the couplings crashing, sparks,
steam, and the massive black hog moaning with effort,
and you still standing there waiting, relaxed looking
but fright and ecstasy washing around in your guts.
The fender comes into focus, the great headlight
beaming down, the heavy groan of the brakes, the red-faced

engineer screaming unheard, swearing, praying, his words
swallowed by the wheels. And two seconds before your death

you step off into the sloping gravel and grasses and roll away
from the sucking wall of wind, feeling the ground trembling
like a girl under your body, the cool of it, the linger of
the train's whistle like a thin violin note coming from a far hill,
fading. Then that long silence after the train passes, where
you lie in the grass beside the tracks feeling the rush
ebb from your body as the grasses calm, and your breath calms,
and a small white butterfly flies in quavery loops
over the jimson weed.

The Physics of Contingency

In strange towns, in the lonely hours of very early
morning and late night, his rig parked outside full
of steel or bananas or felt slippers, he used to call
the tired waitress over and say,
"Watch this."
And though the diner was busy and her feet ached,
she'd stand in her green poly apron and watch him because of
the little smile curling the corners of his mouth
and because he was so curiously focused, intent as
a surgeon as he poured a few grains of salt on the counter,
scraped them together in a thin line, and then slowly put
the salt shaker down, so delicately... delicately...
at a 45° angle against the grains, and held it there with
three fingers, reverently as a jeweler holding the Koh-i-Noor,
while he gently blew away the salt from the base of the shaker.
The waitress would stand beguiled. Two fingers. One.
He'd let go.
And his salt shaker would lean at 45 on a few invisible
crystals of salt, holding steady its precarious balance
in the uncertain world of commerce and uneasy eggs.
Delighted he would grin at the waitress.
Delighted she would grin back at him.

In Recovery

I was scraping carrots at the table.
You were filing the brass of a knife hilt.
Whenever you paused your rasping,
we could hear the sleet whispering down
through the dead oak leaves. It was dark outside,
and we were at peace and safe in the warm kitchen.

We were talking about the weather
and you told me the coldest you had ever been
was coming back from an overdose. Your friends
had packed your groin in ice, brought you back
to the cruel light and unendurable cold, you said.
"Unbelievable cold. I was cold to my core," you said.
"Cold. Cold."
I asked you how it was to come back
and you said, "Oh, it was no big deal. I mean,"
you said, "I didn't give it much thought."
Then you smiled faintly and added,
"And then, believe it, I dressed and went out
to score some more."

We thought for awhile. We talked about Iraq
and we talked about a guy we knew who
got on disability after years of trying and died
two weeks later, and we wondered about whether
baked or mashed with our fried chicken, and

you said your next knife handle would be
desert ironwood.

Next morning under a sharp and brilliant blue sky
the snow lay along the branches of the ginkgo
like long albino snakes.
Smoke rose like the flume of white whales
from the chimneys of the snow-humped roofs.
Blackbirds fluttered and swooped in the snow—
motes in a blind eye.

We drank our coffee and looked out.
"But what was it like to O.D., what was that like
to be almost dead?"

"Which time?" you said.

The Sum of a Man

In autumn,
facing the end of his life,
he moved in with me.
We piled his belongings—
his army-issue boots, knife magazines,
Steely Dan tapes, his grinder, drill press,
sanders, belts and hacksaws—
in a heap all over the living room floor.
For two weeks he walked around the mess.

One night he stood looking down at it all
and said: "The sum total of my existence."
Emptiness in his voice.

Soon after, as if the sum total
needed to be expanded, he began to place
things around in the closets and spaces I'd
cleared for him, and when he'd finished
setting up his workshop in the cellar, he said,
"I should make as many knives as I can,"
and he began to work.

The months plowed on through a cold winter.
In the evenings, we'd share supper, some tale
of family, some laughs, perhaps a walk in the snow.
Then he'd nip back down into the cellar's keep
to saw and grind and polish,
creating his beautiful knives

until he grew too weak to work.
But still he'd slip down to stand at his workbench
and touch his woods
and run his hand over his lathe.

One night he came up from the cellar
and stood in the kitchen's warmth
and, shifting his weight
from one foot to the other, said,
"I love my workshop."
Then he went up to bed.

He's gone now.
It's spring. It's been raining for weeks.
I go down to his shop and stand in the dust
of ground steel and shavings of wood.
I think on how he'd speak of his dying, so
easily, offhandedly, as if it were
a coming anniversary or
an appointment with the moon.
I touch his leather apron, folded for all time,
and his glasses set upon his work gloves.
I take up an unfinished knife and test its heft,
and feel as well the heft of my grief for
this man, this brother I loved,
the whole of him so much greater
than the sum of his existence.

Say Goodbye, Say It Without Angels

He lies thin as a wafer on his bed
all white in the light of morning,
sleeping.
Sunken lids purple as petals,
nose sharp and thin as a thorn.
I lean against the door and watch him,
waiting for the next rising of his chest.
I wait a long while before he draws in
a long harsh breath, like hauling
a rusted bucket up from a deep well.
I breathe in then, too.
A few tears of relief.
Yet one hour, I know, I will watch
the life go out of him.

I see the future and it is an immense
and empty sky that goes on and on,
bluer and bluer, higher and wider,
spectacular in its purity and vacancy,
cold and terrifying in its silence.

I will stand on the edge, Michael,
I will stand on the edge and call to you,
and listen to the silence of your answer.

In a Blind Hour

I was glad he was still sleeping, and I took
my coffee into the living room and began
to read the poems aloud—practicing wise,
practicing melancholy, practicing wit—
until I heard him struggling upstairs
and even then, I read one more poem.

When then I went up, he said angrily,
"Look what I coughed up." And I saw
he had hemorrhaged.
He bathed himself and I
got him to come down where he sat on the couch
and took a little coffee and a few drags on
a cigarette. I called the ambulance.

When they arrived, he said,
"I'll get dressed." No, he was told,
it would not be necessary for him to get dressed.
He considered this. Then he said, patiently,
"I won't go out of here without my pants on."
He put his jeans on and a clean shirt,
and he put his cigarettes, a new pack of gum
and his glasses in the shirt pocket, and he
smoothed back his hair with the palms of his hands.
Then he told the medics who were waiting there—
incurious, impassive, their radios crackling
and wheezing in the silence—

"Don't bring that thing in here," meaning
the stretcher, and he walked by himself down
the front stairs and out to the curb to where
the ambulance hummed and the red light pulsed.
They strapped him up.
I leaned to him to say, "I'll be there right after
the reading."

Only then did the serene matter-of-factness
he'd held to since his diagnosis
leave him and, his voice breaking, he asked,
"And you'll take me home?" The tears just there.
And I said,
"We'll see."

I said, "We'll see."
Not, "Yes, yes, my brother,
I will take you home again."
I said, "We'll see."
They closed the doors
and the ambulance rolled down the street
and turned left at the corner under the sycamore.

And I turned to the Library where
all the people were waiting I could not disappoint.
I read my careful poems, I schmoozed,
drank punch, sold books.
After the party, I drove to the hospital.

In the corner of a room greying with the dusk,
a big sparse room, three other beds empty,
I found him.
His lids fluttered when I called out to him,
but he did not wake to me.
He was making a noise in his throat—
En en en en en en en en—
not a noise but a note starting high and falling
to a sigh, like a lone bird in a dark forest
singing of night coming down.
He sang his simple song all night
until, towards dawn, it guttered in his throat.

He never came back to me.

One day I told a friend of my anguish
at not telling Michael I would bring him home.
He would not have felt so abandoned.
The friend said, "But would you have wanted
the last thing you said to your brother
to be a lie?"

Sophist!
Ape of wisdom!
Jesuitic pimp!
My heart's in its cave in hell.

What Is Lost

I say, "I lost my brother in April."
Lost.
As if, if I looked hard enough—in his workshop,
down Home Depot's aisles, in the woods—
I'd find him again.

Sometimes I'll think I see his lanky body
loping down Grove Street, his hands
jammed in his pockets, his black cap,
the lilt in his feet,
or I'll see him passing me in the cab of his Kenworth
heading south on I-95.
I see him some evenings through the foggy
smokeshop window picking up his Pall Malls.
I see him by the misting Ten Mile River
with his traps and his dog.
I see him. I see him.

I don't cry for him. I look for him.
He never comes home.

Catullus says, "What you see is lost, set down as lost."

In this morning's fog, in front of the steel company's
old brick front, they cut down the three elegant firs
that glittered in the rain and housed the birds.
I watched until they took the tops

and fed them to the chipper.
I stood and stared at the big empty hole
where they had been.
Then I went around to the back of the building
where the trains pick up steel headed for Weirton,
and I leaned against the skids of coils
and I wept.

Prayer for my Brother

I hope all your highs were beautiful.

I hope the rapture threading through your cells
    each time you eased the iron needle in
    was worth long years of ordinary life.

I hope the sounds of the moth pattering the light bulb,
    the faucet's silver drip,
    Buddy Guy singing "Feels like Rain" on the radio
    pulled you whole into harmony's sweet sphere.

I hope you felt light as thistle seed, warm as inside a woman,
    tranquil as the night laid out in stars over the Woonasquatucket.

I hope the Mexican Horse rode away with all your pain.

I hope that brown sugar satisfied your hunger for all
    the love you longed for and should have had.

I hope your golden visions made possible for you a world of
    all-shall-be-well.

I hope the poppy's grace allowed you, if only for the
    minutes of a nod, a means to love your shy uncertain soul.

I hope the brave animal of your heart grew big enough
    to fill that hollow of despair.

I hope Golden Girl held you
　　for as long as you wanted
　　before she rocked you home.

I hope you saw God.

I hope his eyes were kind.

Pleasure Beach

In October, I took his ashes to the Sound.
I carried him jetty to jetty three miles to
Pleasure Beach where the deserted houses were,
where sands buried the front steps
and small boats lay down on their sides.
The only life around was the occasional odd rabbit or gull.
He had loved this little ghost town.
While he was dying, he would come here
and spend the day wandering.
He had called it "the vestibule to eternity's ballroom."
Then he'd grin.

I carried him this grey day down the single street
past the empty houses and cabins, their frayed curtains
drifting out of broken windows on a breeze,
lawn mowers and hammocks rusting on the lawns.
A child's swing creaked in the wind and
from somewhere the faint tinkling of wind chimes.
Otherwise, all silence, all peace.

I carried him to where the road crumbled off into weed.
I carried him through the fields of beard grass and sedge
to where two huge radio towers rose up from scrub pines
to straddle the narrow peninsula in the harbor.
The towers' red lights blinked softly in the fog.
It began to rain, but it was an October rain and warm.
I carried him across from the inlet side to the open Sound.

The rain was steady now,
the grey waves grinding in.

I was searching for a special place to leave him.
I tramped through hummocks of beach grass
and clumps of rusting beach plum. I examined
the cave under a crumbling basement. I looked
under the two granite benches on the bluff
and sat on one and looked out at the sea.
The rain came harder, and I was weeping,
it was so beautiful—the white feathered waves,
the rain, the wide and silvered sky—and
it was so lonely.
I turned from the wind
and took him home.

Jim

Jimmie and the Moongirl

We were twelve.
Midsummer nights in the old schoolyard,
sweetgrass growing up from cracks in the asphalt,
honeysuckle melting in the hot air,
we'd gather under the naked white moon
to chase the fireflies drifting in the dark, fairy lights pulsing.
Swatting one another, giggling, we'd run in lazy circles,
the boys slyly trying to touch, without seeming to,
a small bird breast, a willow waist. The girls would scatter
shrieking, then turn like Bacchantes to fire at their heads
the hard-as-marbles unripe grapes growing on the old chain fence.

We threw out bad words—*cootchie, balls, hump, hickey*—
our hearts hammering with dare and dread.
On a bet once, the Hebert boys brought out their
pale penises—delicate as night blooming moonvine,
boneless as albino garden slugs—
and peed on the school wall below the principal's window.
The girls screeched and loathed, but stole their furtive looks.

One girl was not afraid. A head taller than any of us,
long gold legs and breasts like honeydews, Sandy,
grave and kind, would take the boys by the hand to the
leaf-shaded streetlight, unbutton her blouse and show herself.
"Touch my titties," she'd invite, smiling like a saint in rapture,
"You can touch them if you like."

Laughing, shouldering one another,
the boys would line up to just barely graze a breast
as if it were a sleeping marmot.

Only Jimmie, waiting to be last, came to her calmly,
and even though the boys danced behind singing, moaning,
"Oh, Jimmie, oh yeah, Jimmie, do it, do it, Ja-Ja-Jimmie,"
he took her hand as if they were all alone in the world
and led her away from the light to the dusty maples
at the schoolyard's edge.
He stroked her breasts slowly and reverently.
He took his time. Her silk nipples changed into
something like the shape of gum drops.
He opened his fist where three fireflies were blinking their last.
He whispered something to her. Then he crumbled their amber
abdomens with his forefinger and, intent as Vermeer,
painted the paste of their gold phosphor on Sandy's nipples.

All that evening she moved enchanted among us,
bare breasted, luminous as those plastic angels
that glowed in the dark of our childhood
so we would not be afraid.

Jimmie Full in the Belly

Every Monday afternoon
after school lets out
you'll see him, quick and feral,
slip into the alley off Hallett Street,
drop his books in the dirt and,
skinny as he is, slide between
the chained gates of the small stockade
that hides the dead flowers and trash
of Saints Cyril & Methodius Church.
Bent over the pit like an old augur,
he'll be culling the ashes for coins
from the burnt Sunday Offering envelopes,
sifting and picking with blackened fingers,
gleaning the penny, nickel, dime
the sexton missed.

When he finds what he can,
he'll lope home to Father Panik Village
where in the basement dark
he'll scrub the black coins with
an old toothbrush and vinegar until
they gleam like wolves' teeth.
Then in the growing dusk, spray bottle
of ammonia tucked in his pants
(defense against the older toughs),
he'll run across the blacktop yards
to Schwartel's Grocer where

for 10 cents a pound, he'll buy as many
bananas as the coins will pay for,
as many as eight or nine sometimes,
and, careful to be alone, bananas stuffed
in his shirt, he'll make his way down to the
ferry landing at Bridgeport Harbor.

Beneath the P.T. Barnum Bridge,
he'll wedge himself between
the green pilings and dark rocks
and slowly peel
and slowly eat
one gold meaty banana after another,
while the ferry, tipsy daytrippers on deck,
glides in all lit up like a party.

Fly Fishing

He sat in the van watching the boats,
watching the egrets, watching the sky.
A black fly crept around the rim
of his plastic mug, ventured down the inside,
was caught in the beer foam, slid in.
"Shit," the man said calmly. An observation.
He watched the fly battle the bubbles.
Eventually the foam subsided and the fly
swam in clear gold beer.
"Shit," he said again. He watched it struggle
until finally it expired, flattened, floated
motionless on the gold.

The man was still.

After some time, he poked his finger in the beer
until the fly adhered. He brought it up on his
forefinger and laid it delicately on the dashboard.
He rummaged in the glove compartment for
packets of salt, opened them with his teeth,
poured the salt in a mound on the dead fly.
Then he sat back and watched the boats,
the egrets and the sky.

Two, three minutes passed. The man leaned forward,
gently he blew the salt away.
The fly, uncovered, staggered up, washed its face

with its two front legs, and flew shakily out the window. "Shit," the man said.

He turned the radio low, sat back.

He finished his beer.

Marlboro Van Man

In the van
he shakes tobacco from the can
onto old newspaper in his lap,
rakes it with a matchbook cover
into a neat rick,
with his forefinger makes
a trench in the Zig-Zag paper,
pinches the tobacco up
with a hand as steady as he can manage,
sows it in the paper's gulley,
tamps it, rolls it, licks it, lights it,
sucks the smoke deep, deep, holds it,
exhales slowly, seriously, reverently
as if breathing Life into the Void.

Buddha in the Bottle, Buddha in the Van

Today
the man in the van did not come out.
He pulled the little gray curtains he
crocheted last winter across the van's windows.
He lay all day in the dark on his mat,
sipping from time to time The Swede's
homemade glögg.
He pondered things.

The day passed.
Big clouds, white and silent,
drifted over him.
Gulls glided by and shat on his hood.
Dogs barked far away,
gnats hung in pools of warm air,
and the green river flowed on and on.
The man kept silence
in the dark of the van.

Night came and brought
a light rain.
The man lay and listened.

He Is The River

He lives by the tides.
He heralds the herons, the green legged ones.
He searches the grey swells
   for the shining grey heads of the seals
   that swim upriver with the Sound's tide.
He blesses the deer swimming across
   to Nell's Island, heads high,
   antlers gleaming.
He mothers mallards,
   watching over the nest of buff eggs
   the foolish hen produced
   by the edge of the road.
He hails the hardy fishing boat, the old grey
   oysterboat, the massive barge.
He marks the wild and sullen
   waterspout that funnels up to the clouds.
He grins at this reversal of gravity.
He witnesses the double rainbows over the river
   merging and separating their jeweled mists.
He applauds the cormorant flying over the
   low tide flats, a muscular eel in its beak
   whipping and thrashing, their wild erratic flight.
He notes the speck of a hawk roaming the high blue sky,
   watches it rocket down to the pigeon on the road,
   the sudden blast of feathers and dirt.
He salutes the skedaddler pigeon walking in
   dizzy circles, its head going very fast in and out,

    settling its feathers and resettling its feathers.
He approves of the swan's easy white indolence.
He admires the ferocity of the blue and green
    crabs he nets, their mad stalk eyes.
He laughs at the small green parakeets
    darting in and out of the swamp pines
    like minnows in green water.
He sleeps with his head out his van window
    to smell low tide, consider the stars.
He rises each morning just before light,
    pees on the beech plum, takes his pole to
    the lip of the river, casts, brings in a few shad
    and several snappers, fries them in corn oil
    and eats them—so becoming slightly more shad
    and more snapper.

He stands in a light mist where the small waves
    slosh up to the boat ramp.
He belches.
He says, "Thank you."
He studies the soft orange rays of the sun
    as they seep up from the dark trees across the river.
He greets the hard-eyed gulls.
He heralds the white herons.
He bows to the rolling blue river.
He lives by its tides.

A Good Day

The man in the old maroon van
boiled his coffee on a tiny burner.
He stirred it with an old stick of
licorice. While he drank, he smoked.
He considered the white smoke
as it flowed and spiraled sideways
in the early light.

He combed his hair with his fingers
and knotted it in a matador's bun.
He spit on his hand and smoothed
his white beard.
Then he climbed down from his van
carrying an onion with long limp shoots
and three soft eyed potatoes.
In his garden—an old dirt-filled wooden
rowboat near the pines—he planted
the onion and the three potatoes
among his lilies and elephant ears.

He went down to the river's edge carrying his pole.
Bonesy, Richie and The Swede
shared their beer with him.
They ate the potato chips—breakfast.
Then they sat all the day fishing, smoking,
talking low.
No one caught anything.
No one was unhappy.

The river turned silver to blue to gray
as the sun rolled from one shore to the other.
He watched the fishing boats
come chugging back in the dusk,
and the tide rose smooth and steady.
He witnessed the moon haul herself up
from the dark marshes.
Bonesy, Richie and The Swede took up
their poles and went home.
He climbed the hill to his van
where he sat on the rotted running board
to smoke one last cigarette and watch
the stars creep out like winkles
dragging their shine across the sky.

Lake Lillinonah

Jim and Buddy, 1992

Early summer, night, the walk
across the flatlands pleasant,
wading through the tall grass,
our poles knocking our thighs
and an easing wind carrying
the smell of water from Lake Lillinonah.

We come to the cove, set our lanterns
on old tree roots by the shore,
thread cornmeal balls on hooks
(and eat some—the sweet boiled
honey dough good with beer),
and cast out into the black lake.

Not much talk, an easy hour
casting, sipping, listening to the lake's
silence. Some early gnats, no moon
or carp yet.

Then Buddy says softly, urgently, "Look!"
At first I see some sparkings,
small red glints,
the way lantern light will catch
lake ripples and spark them back.

Then I see. Eyes. They glint
and disappear and glint again, three
pairs of eyes, ten, twenty, more come
swaying, zig-zagging on the water.
"Snakes," Buddy whispers, and throws
a rock. I throw a rock. The snakes whip
and swirl, and the water swirls with them.

"Too many," I say. "Not right," says Buddy.
"This must be some special night," he says.
We go on throwing rocks at the
silent churning in the water
until the night is taken up with snakes,
the lake is full of eyes, and boiling.

When the snakes, ribbons of yellow gleaming
on their thin, brown backs, begin writhing
up on shore, Buddy swears, "Goddamn!"
We grab our lanterns, poles and filleting knives,
leave the cornmeal balls for them,
stumble through the damp eel grass
feeling snakes seeping into our boots,
worming up beneath our pant legs,
dropping around our necks,
coiling in our armpits, slipping their tongues
in our ears—vague, foul, remembered forms

we learned to fear long before
we learned to walk like men.

A white moon rocks out of a black crack
in the sky and we run hunched under its cold light
through the grass and hush of trees
all the way to the long winding road where
a half mile away a semi is growling from 4th to 3rd,
the cab all lit up with white and yellow lights
gay and comforting like town,
like church, like 7-Eleven.
We stand on the road's edge and watch it come on,
loving the truck and the truck's gold lights and
whatever the truck is hauling
and the lone truck driver
and the solid asphalt road.

The Birdcatcher

From the long dark chimney
like out of a tall black hat
the mourning dove explodes into the room
feathering walls, windows, mirrors
with her white whirlings,
her crazy caramboles.
Poofs of soot like magic show smoke
drift down from her wings.
The room fills with her terror.
Shocked shy, old grey cat
backs into the curtain
trying her disappearing act.

Jim hears and hunts the room.
She's on the clock beating time.
Lithe and quick, he leaps
and it's all fingers and feathers
and a heart banging mad to escape.

Jim holds her to his chest.
With his thumb he tucks her head
under her wing, croons,
cradles her upside down, feet straight up.
He shuts her in his hand, winds up,
whirls her round. Three times
she flies the circle in his dark hand.

When he opens up, her abalone eyes are closed.
She lies still as dead.
He studies her—
melon and aqua and buff.
Rusty head. Lavender lids.
Candle-pink feet.
He strokes her beak.
He whispers things.
He smooths her wisteria wings.

He carries her to the door where outside
the sleepy bees are floating and weaving
among the yellow hollyhocks.
Jim holds her out on his open palm,
blows twice on her sleeping head.

The feathers lift on her neck.
Her black eyes open.
She lies a moment, content in his palm.
She rustles. She blinks.
She lifts her wings.
The sky takes her back in.

The Bird

In April there came down the river
a very big black bird.
Each day the bird circled over the dock
in five wide gyres before he lighted on a piling.
Then he'd swash around the dock
looking left and right with black bean eyes.
His wings glistened, iridescent as oil slick.
He had a ring of white feathers around his neck
and a fine white breast.
He was a very big black bird.

He ate leftover bait and emptied the
discarded bags of potato chips.
He tipped up empty beer cans and
drank the last warm drops.
He rattled the trashcans and perturbed the gulls.

Miguel was afraid. He told everyone
a black bird was bad luck.
But Jim The Van Man told Miguel
the bird was not evil.
He had that white feathered torque
and the white breast shield—
the sign of gods.

The Van Man began to talk to the bird.
He would tell the bird he was a little bugger and

his parents must have been big buggers.
Jim and the bird watched the river's moods,
listened to the dockies' stories, shared fish and pizza.
The bird let Jim stroke him all over.
And the bird Jim named Oreo
learned to sit on his shoulder
so, together, facing the sun rising from the wetlands,
they looked like some otherworldly two-headed god.

Last Tuesday Jim was sitting up in his van
watching the bird stomp around on the hood
when the bird sidled in and perched on his steering wheel.
The bird had moved in.

Until one night a man came to the dock carrying tethers
and looking for his lost $900 Pied Crow from Africa.
There were mutterings among a few jealous drunks
that Jim stole the bird. It was Fat Slob pointed to the van
and collected $100.

I was lying beside Jimmie listening to music in the van
when the man came banging.
I was the one who handed Oreo over.
Oreo stretched wide his wings like Quetzalcoatl.
The man hooked a leash to the jess.
Jim disappeared.

Those still fishing under the moon
heard the two wild cries that carried from
way behind the hill to the river's edge.
Then silence.
I found Jim back of the hill curled under
the rhododendrons,
hands over his head,
and I held him while he wept.

These days Oreo comes down the river
free flying as before. He'll come to Jim,
but Jim will yell and bang pots and
throw bits of stick. "Fucker," he'll shout,
"Get away, little fucker." And the bird will
get high in the oak and look down
with one eye, then the other.

Rain

She was missing him.
Rain and more rain, and the down-drifting dark.
She went down to the river to find him.
He was not in his van on the little hill.
He was not sitting behind the curtain of rain
on the porch of Brown's Bait & Tackle.
He was not sleeping under the old rotted oysterboat
upended near the transit crane.
She went down to the rickety dock and
walked out on the fingers to peer in each boat.
All were empty, all silent but for the groan and whine
of bumpers rubbing the dock, the drum of the rain on decks,
the slap of waves portside.

She stood and listened, rain seeping down her collar,
runneling into the corners of her mouth.
She lifted her face and stuck out her tongue, curling it
in a furrow. The rain tasted slightly like fern.
Then she heard it—thin music twining with the wind
coming from the east side of Cappy's houseboat.
She walked carefully—for the river was swamping the planks—
out to the dock's last finger where she found
the dwarfed *Freebird* rolling in place on the other side
of the trawler *Stacey Frances*.

She called to him. She called three times, the rain
was so loud, before he came up out of the dark cabin and

smiled and held her hand as she climbed in.
He kissed her and gave her a beer and they sat
under the cabin roof eating chips, watching the horizon
blacken and blur.

They watched the *Ganymede* struggle in, watched the men
work to secure her. The *Ganymede* threw her spotlight
on the dark dock. Through that brilliance, the rain fell in long
streams of silver. The men on deck heaved their purple bags
of clams up to the dock where men, gleaming like wet seals,
caught them and stacked them high in the pick-up. Then,
bowed under their hoodies like dark monks, the men ran
from the dock through the rain towards Brown's dim
yellow lights.

And the rain rattled on the cabin roof. They listened awhile
to Neil Young sing "Southern Man."
They watched the high-running river roll and froth,
churning the rain into its belly. Then they scuttled out on deck
and crawled under the stiff heavy tarp that smelled
agreeably of fish and salt and oil. Dark, they could not
see each other's eyes. But they could feel each other's
wet and burning skin, and their breath fell on one another
like incense. Through the canvas, the rain felt like
birdshot on their skin.
They laughed.

It was strange making love on the small rocking boat.
They did not have to try.
They just held each other,
and the *Freebird* rocked them one into the other.

A Woman in Love

A woman in love
is a woman with her feet to the flames,
her hand on a natural heart,
her head in a veil of rain.
She moves like a schooner through
thick waters of continuous desire.
She glides under the grove's green light
gathering quince for her beloved.
She hums above the fire
while the love feast smokes and boils.
She dances slowly and seriously
to late night radio love songs,
her hips riding tides, her belly
revolving around her marble navel.
Her love sits beside the one candle,
smoking, watching her. His eyes
gleam in the dark. The smoke curls
round and up from his fingers.

Touched by her man,
the skin of a woman in love
will ache, and the small hairs
on her forearm lean towards him.
Her breasts grow taut and proud,
her nipples shine like the pink noses
of baby rabbits.

The hand of a woman in love
touches his as if she were touching
electrified water—his current
flowing into her, their hands
roaming together through magnetic fields.
When he draws the tip of his finger down
the pale orb of her belly,
small blue sparks jump up
like flowers in a field.
He gathers them.

The eyes of a woman in love
grow blacker and deeper
as he comes to her. And when
her eyes are as black and deep as wells,
he falls into them.

I Lie in Wonder

I lie in wonder some nights,
my eyes open to the dark,
thinking you must have a secret religion,
you must be a Theravadin monk,
when sometimes you kiss my nipples
hard as little thimbles,
stroke all of me that is creviced and cleft,
search the swirls of my ears with your slow tongue,
and at just that rapt agony of pre-coming,
you stop, whisper *Love,* and hold me
    saying
        This is all. Just the touch. This is enough.
You hold me hard until my body stops
its trembling and bucking, until, stilled and cooling
and coming back from the wilderness of the
surrendered self, I understand what it is
to be the flame the white mist settles over—
    all opaque, but lit within.

West Wind

There is a wind tonight.
The road to the river is bordered on one side
by fieldstone, on the other by war wire
to protect the fancy yachts. I hike past these
to come to the unfenced part, the common route,
where tonight everything—trees, rushes, sedge,
goldenrod, woolgrass—is moving in the wind.
The trees' shadows on the road are swaying and
swirling, so the road moves too. The waters move
in a million silver circles on the river's surface.
There is a crooked half-moon. Around it, the thin
clouds move like water flowing over the moon and
around it. The moon rests in the coursing clouds like
a white stone in a river.

There is some bird. I cannot see the bird, but
it keeps crying through the dark. It's a high, sad calling,
like an infant abandoned in the reeds.
Two fishermen stand very still on the dock beside
their lanterns. The many long spun clouds on the river's
horizon are moving east, and the river moves east too,
so the fishermen appear to be gliding effortlessly west,
being ferried to where the sun has flamed out.

I find Jim up on the hill tending to his vodka.
In his head he is somewhere else, but he invites me
to sit out with him on the old junk car seat under

the cottonwood. He offers, I take, a sip from his bottle.
I say something about the nightbird, he says something
about the herring, I say moon, he says world.
"I have the whole world in my hands," he says,
"and when I go, it goes." I laugh.
Jim goes somewhere else again, his eyes moving up
to the tree, intent, staring as if he can see the spirit
of the wind diddling the leaves.
He comes back.
"Don't laugh," he smiles sadly, "I am wise beyond my means."
We sit in silence then, watching leaves flutter and
twirl on their stems. We watch the two delicate bats
flickering and swooping around the dark hill and
the occasional ghost moth tossed sideways by the wind.

I consider Jim's idea—the world is our mind's artifice.
He'd say, Be kind, and welcome what you look upon.
It is all you.
Jim slips to sleep. I kiss his head and take the bottle
from his hands and place it on the ground.
The wind's picked up. I pull his old towel to his chin
and turn towards home.
The world is all around in motion and
the world's in me.
Praise be.

St. Valentine's Day

My father was unable to hug me
or talk to me. He could never say
"I love you." He was too shy.
Too, his mind was in
another world.
But whenever he came home from his journeys,
he'd bring me presents—Little Lady Toilet Water,
that grand midnight blue Stetson,
those many Waterman and Parker pens,
the pocketbook with the brass eagle clasp.
And for all occasions, overblown cards
with the puffy scented satin heart or rose
on the front. Inside, his scraggy signature,
"To my Paddy, from her Daddy."

When you did not give me
a Valentine today,
I was undone.
And I wept in the shower
even though I am an adult and know
gifts are materialistic shallow
commercially driven wasteful crap.

But why, why could you not have
wasted some mute love on me?

Not Happiness but Something Else

My daughter feels bad
that I am with the man I'm with.
"I wish more for you," she says.
She means his angers, his drinking, his paranoias.
His other-side-of-the-tracks.
"I know," I say. "Don't worry. I have
a rich inner life." She smiles.
"I just want you to be happy," she says.
I tell her happiness isn't everything.
And I think about how the man
is in my life like the wild green parrot,
the two stray cats, the lame squirrel almost tame—
we are not the same species,
but they are warm
and need saving.

His Anger

They are talking, sitting in the kitchen, having
tea, perhaps, or wine, looking at one another
with love. It happens in a second. It happens
in the middle of her smile,
it happens as slowly as a silver water drop swells,
elongates, as fast as it falls from the faucet to the pan.
Some word she says, some way of saying that word,
some glance away, some angle of her chin,
and that wild, hard look comes into his eye,
a chill around his lips,
the awful look of dignity about him,
his drawing away one cold inch at a time,
drawing up taller, pulling the heat
of his anger inside.

What is it? What is it? What have I said?
Cold drifts down between them
like breath in zero weather,
and she knows that soon, minutes maybe,
he'll take the key off his key ring and
lay it on the table, he'll be putting his things
in his van, his silence like a beating,

and she'll sit still as a stone carving,
her hands around her skull,
trying to breathe,
trying to swallow the thick spit of fear,
trying to freeze the tears that enrage him so,

trying to speak, the enormous effort to move her tongue,
to make him understand: "Forgive me, please,
you have to forgive me," for whatever it was
angered him, for whatever it was he thought
she harmed him by.

The Spell

She knows he's bad for her—
his drinking, his rages,
how she's gone for so many days
with ache in her heart from some hurt
he's inflicted, or some hurt of his own
that she suffers for him.

He keeps her in silence.
He keeps her canted on a tilted ground.
He keeps her thirsting by the pool of lovingkindness.
She keeps him keeping her there.

She loves him.
"What is this, then, that I love him?" she begs
of a friend. She cries to the friend,
"We have nothing in common!"

"Yes, you do," says the friend—
"Suffering."

One Man

I have seen a man, intent and patient, cup
a fledgling and feed it tenderly with a straw.
The man would hum softly, a one-note song,
when he did this.

I've seen a man bring raw steak to the dock
to throw high in the air to the starving
hawk with the bad leg.

I've seen a man teach a crow to hold a cigarette
in one claw and eat peanut butter from the tip
so the crow would seem to be smoking.
He would laugh when he did this.

I've seen a man whistle to the pigeons to flock on
the hood of his van when he parked at the water's edge.
The hood would be purple with pigeons.
He'd feed them millet and old donuts.

And I've seen a man in a blaze of drunken rage at me
crush to death the little green parrot I loved.

And it was the same man.

Ice

It is the dead of winter,
and the ninth day of no word from you.
I am filled with the sick dread
that you have left without a word,
gone back to your old world of drifting.
I go down to the river
to stand with your ghost by the shore.

The gulls are huddled here, all facing west.
A pale sun lends each gull a bluish shadow.
The whole world is ice, rock, river.
Three o' clock. The *Gypsy,* last of the oysterboats
to come in, has been unloaded, the oystermen gone off
to Lavery's bar for beer and warmth.
You used to go with them, but not for warmth.

The river's broad back is smooth as metal plate,
but underneath a strong current roils,
moving the mass of small ice floes downriver.
The ice hisses and rustles as its riddled edges
mesh and un-mesh. From the dock,
hundreds of floes on the move give me
the dizzying feeling that it is the dock and I
that plow the river. "Our own little johnboat,"
you used to say, happy to own nothing.
On shore, great piled slabs of ice like

tectonic plates are angled this way and that—
a white wreck of a world.

Way upriver near Derby Dam the larger ice
blocks are unlocking.
Their gun-crack and deep boom echo along the banks.
Barge-sized floes the color of alabaster
free themselves.
Most move heavily out to the river's center,
drift leisurely down through Milford,
pick up speed in Stratford, make knots toward the mouth.
But some catch a cowlick current and circle dockwards.
They move, slow and relentless, towards the pilings.
One floe rams with an explosive crackling and
grinding. The dock rocks.
I keep my balance.
The grey-green pilings moan and lurch and sway,
but hold.

Among an argosy of smaller floes advancing,
six turn out to be swans.
Blue-white, their wings raised like sails,
necks taut, heads high, looking neither
to the right nor to the left, the swans
float swiftly with the floes. Ice swans.
Which one is you, my swain, my shapeshifter drifter?

The surprise of them, the beauty of them
does not move me.
I am not consoled.
You are gone, and I am bound by heart
to your river,
to your cold world.
Enduring.

About the Author

Norah Pollard lives by the Housatonic River, which keeps her afloat spiritually; works by day at a Bridgeport steel company, which keeps her grounded; and shares the spirit of her father, Red Pollard, which keeps her flying on Pegasus just as he flew on Seabiscuit. At various points in her life she has been a folk-singer, seam-stitcher, nanny, teacher, solderer, and print shop calligrapher. She received the Academy of American Poets Prize from the University of Bridgeport, and for several years edited *The Connecticut River Review*. Pollard's two poetry collections, *Leaning In* and *Report from the Banana Hospital*, were published in 2003 and 2005. She has had a life-long passion for the visual arts, which she has put to good use as an editor-designer and illustrator. Norah Pollard lives in Stratford, Connecticut, with her cats Lilybeet and Phoenix.

Colophon

Death & Rapture in the Animal Kingdom is set largely in Garamond Premier Pro, which had its genesis in 1988 when type-designer Robert Slimbach visited the Plantin-Moretus Museum in Antwerp, Belgium, to study its collection of Claude Garamond's metal punches and typefaces. In the mid-1500's Garamond, a Parisian punch-cutter, produced a refined array of book types that combined an unprecedented degree of balance and elegance, for centuries standing as the pinnacle of beauty and practicality in type-founding. Slimbach has created an entirely new interpretation based on Garamond's designs and on comparable italics cut by Robert Granjon, Garamond's contemporary. Titles are set in Felix Titling, a font based closely on an alphabet developed by the Veronese calligrapher and painter, Felice Feliciano, which appeared in 1463 in his treatise on Roman inscriptions. The original is preserved in the Vatican library.

To order additional copies of
Death & Rapture in the Animal Kingdom
or other Antrim House titles, contact the publisher at

Antrim House
PO Box 111, Tariffville, CT 06081
860.217.0023, AntrimHouse@comcast.net
or the house website (www.AntrimHouseBooks.com).

•

On the house website
are sample poems, upcoming events,
and a "seminar room" featuring discussion topics
& writing suggestions offered by Antrim House authors
as well as supplemental biography, notes, images and poems.